D0187895

# OFFICIAL RECORD OF * EASILY OVER-LOOKED EVERYDAY DETAILS

*

**IAM**

Name..............................

Address............................

....................................

Phone..............................

E-mail.............................

IF FOUND PLEASE RETURN TO:

P·5821-474

# I WAS HERE

a travel journal for the curious minded

created & illustrated by
Kate Pocrass

CHRONICLE BOOKS
SAN FRANCISCO

SERIE 1

028

Copyright © 2011 by Kate Pocrass.
All rights reseved.  No part of this book may be reproduced
in any form without written permission from the publisher.

ISBN:
978-0-8118-7770-1

Manufactured in China

Designed by Kate Pocrass

10 9 8

Chronicle Books LLC
680 Second Street
San Francisco, CA 94107
www.chroniclebooks.com

# CONTENTS
## a handy list of what's inside

# CREDO

## & thougts
## on exploring
## in general

What are the moments that make up a quintessential trip?

All too often people travel the way they think they're supposed to, rushing past the minutiae of daily life without contemplation. Whether I'm reminiscing about my last excursion abroad or remembering my most recent visit to the corner store, the moments I recall are similar. The time en route to a destination and the interactions I have along the way are usually much more memorable than the stopping place.

As you thumb through this journal, you'll find suggestions for urban exploration and the recording of easily overlooked everyday details. This journal will act as your field guide for expeditions near or far. You don't have to travel to exotic faraway lands to notice things along your usual path. Anywhere can be a starting place. Whether in your backyard or overseas, you can still find wonder in the smallest, unexpected details.

The following pages offer space to plan, document while en route, and keep track of important details for subsequent visits. Pages for lists will prompt you to record certain aspects of your trip because the particulars of a journey too often go unrecorded. The journal can function as your personal archive, standing as a testament to any travel adventure.

I encourage you to wander aimlessly, without obligation or pressure. Be guided from one place to the next by instinct. Explore the city and find the extraordinary in the ordinary. Remember to take quiet steps off to the side from your normal path, to pay attention to the peripheries.

– Kate Pocrass

# BEFORE YOU GO

# JUST IN CASE

Emergency Contact: ......................................................

Relation: ......................................................

Phone #: ......................................................

Blood Type: ......................................................

Allergies: ......................................................

Vaccinations: ......................................................

Doctor's Name: ......................................................

Phone #: ......................................................

Health Insurance: ......................................................

Policy #: ......................................................

Phone #: ......................................................

Passport #: ......................................................

Issued By: ......................................................

Credit Card #: ......................................................

If Card Is Lost Call: ......................................................

License #: ......................................................

Car/Moto Plate: ......................................................

......................................................

......................................................

......................................................

......................................................

......................................................

# TO DO BEFORE EMBARKING

- [ ] ......................................................
- [ ] ......................................................
- [ ] ......................................................
- [ ] ......................................................
- [ ] ......................................................
- [ ] ......................................................
- [ ] ......................................................
- [ ] ......................................................
- [x] MAKE A PILE OF ITEMS I WANT TO BRING ALONG
- [x] PUT A THIRD OF THOSE ITEMS AWAY
- [x] PACK THE REST
- [ ] ......................................................
- [ ] ......................................................
- [ ] ......................................................
- [ ] ......................................................
- [ ] ......................................................
- [ ] ......................................................
- [ ] ......................................................
- [ ] ......................................................
- [ ] ......................................................
- [ ] ......................................................
- [ ] ......................................................
- [ ] ......................................................
- [ ] ......................................................
- [ ] ......................................................
- [ ] ......................................................
- [ ] ......................................................

PACKING CHECKLIST

☐ ...................................... ☐ ......................................
☐ ...................................... ☐ ......................................
☐ ...................................... ☐ ......................................
☐ ...................................... ☐ ......................................
☐ ...................................... ☐ ......................................
☐ ...................................... ☐ ......................................
☐ ...................................... ☐ ......................................
☐ ...................................... ☐ ......................................
☐ ...................................... ☐ ......................................
☑ MY FAVORITE PEN .................... ☐ ......................................
☑ SENSE OF WONDER ................... ☐ ......................................
☐ ...................................... ☐ ......................................
☐ ...................................... ☐ ......................................
☐ ...................................... ☐ ......................................
☐ ...................................... ☐ ......................................

## SO & SO TOLD ME    I MUST SEE THE...

## SO & SO TOLD ME    TO AVOID THE...

DRAW SOMETHING HERE & CREATE A CUSTOM POSTCARD

SEND TO:

A GOOD SPOT FOR POSTAGE

STAMP

# SEND LOVE VIA POSTCARDS TO

Name: ................................................
Street: ................................................
City/Zip: ................................................

Name: ................................................
Street: ................................................
City/Zip: ................................................

Name: ................................................
Street: ................................................
City/Zip: ................................................

Name: ................................................
Street: ................................................
City/Zip: ................................................

Name: ................................................
Street: ................................................
City/Zip: ................................................

Name: ................................................
Street: ................................................
City/Zip: ................................................

Name: ................................................
Street: ................................................
City/Zip: ................................................

COLEC
10 C
1
Serie
2

# JOURNEYS

## & things to do while out and about

45596

Find a good, clear map of your surroundings. Following the lines of the city streets, write out your name on the map. Explore this path as your first itinerary.

Wander around a commercial district. Collect
typographic specimens by photographing various
sources that you pass by:

- ☐ store signage
- ☐ license plates
- ☐ doorways
- ☐ monuments
- ☐ street names

If text doesn't thrill you, pick a color and photograph
only instances of that color along your path.

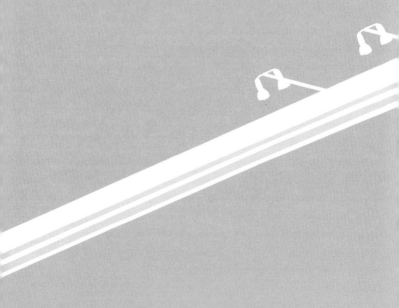

Such YELLOW BRIGHT

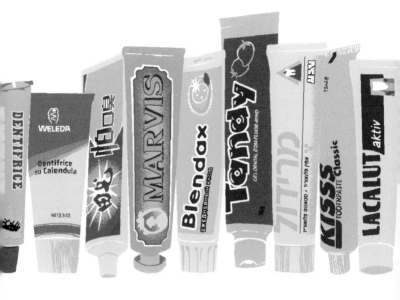

At a local convenience store,
purchase a toiletry brand that you
do not recognize. Start a collection
of this particular item and search
for more on future trips you take.
Treat them as your souvenirs.

For one day, shoot all photos from hip height
without looking through the viewfinder.

TURKISH
TEAPOT

NAMIBIAN
GREASE SPLATTER
GUARD

Purchase an ordinary, everyday,
not-so-fancy kitchen item that
you will use on a regular basis when
you return home. It will serve as a
daily reminder of your travels.

When in a restaurant, take time while perusing the menu. Always ask the server if there is an item you should not miss. Order two dishes: the one you find most appealing and the one you find most unappetizing. The unusual items are often the tastiest.

SUZHOU
YANGCHENG LAKE
HAIRY CRAB

Scour the area for insider information:

- ☐ Gather local weekly papers and check out event listings.
- ☐ Find people in a shop you are interested in and ask for their suggestions of places to check out.
- ☐ Talk to taxi drivers. They often know history and current hot spots by default.
- ☐ Get perfect one-day itineraries from flight attendants.

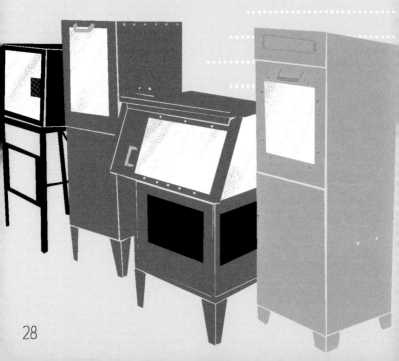

Choose a particular subject matter
for your trip and search for traces of it.

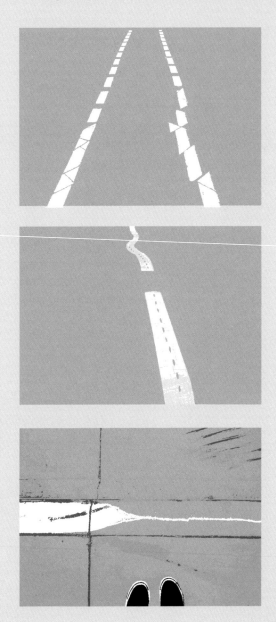

Fig. 1 –
ROAD & SIDEWALK PAINT GONE AWRY

CAULIFLOWER

FENNEL

CELERY

MUSHROOM

Fig. 2 –
TREES THAT LOOK LIKE GIANT VEGETABLES

BAMBOO DISTRICT
FOR BUILDING &
CONSTRUCTION

ANTIQUATED
ELECTRONICS
SWAP MEET

VINTAGE
TABLEWARE
SPECIALIST

FABRIC & TRIM
DISTRICTS

Check out utilitarian areas of town
and districts specializing in one
particular item. This will usually bring
you to areas full of locals and places
most guidebooks do not focus on.

Take time to stare out the window.
Whether in an airplane, bus, or subway car, being on the move
gives you a fresh perspective on everything around you.

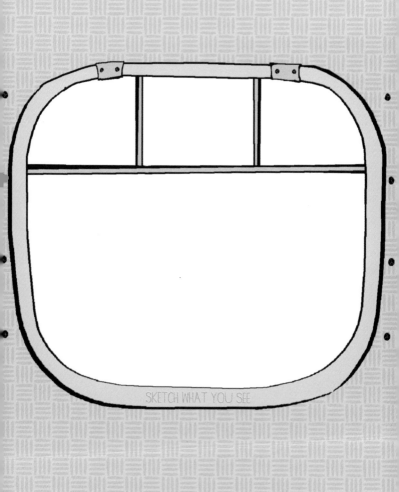

SKETCH WHAT YOU SEE

Search out local versions of establishments you would ordinarily frequent at home. If you feel like being pampered, research forms of grooming specific to where you are instead of spa treatments you can get at home.

CLEAN SHAVE AT
THE NEIGHBORHOOD
BARBER

CHINESE HEAD
MASSAGE &
EAR CLEANING

VENIK FOR A
RUSSIAN BATH

HEATED MARBLE
IN THE TURKISH BATH

ICELANDIC
GEOTHERMAL
SALTWATER
SOAK

Tourist attractions are plentiful and crowded, but embrace it. They are famous for a reason. List the top attractions in the city you are visiting. Pick a few and go during off hours or when they are closed. Sit outside the sites and notice all the things that people hustling inside miss out on.

19TH CATHEDRAL
WE'VE BEEN TO THIS WEEK

BEAUTY & AWE
OVERSATURATION

Find a bustling street corner. Search for a place that you can stay put for about an hour. Record the behavior of several passersby. What color are most people wearing? How quickly or slowly are they walking? In what direction are most people headed?

If someone is talking on their cell phone, try to transcribe the conversation. Record snippets here, filling in what you imagine the person on the other line is saying.

Write a press release or make a flyer about your day.

WHO:
.......................................................................
WHERE:
.......................................................................
WHEN:
.......................................................................
HIGHLIGHTS:
.......................................................................

.......................................................................

.......................................................................

.......................................................................

.......................................................................

.......................................................................

.......................................................................

.......................................................................

.......................................................................

.......................................................................

.......................................................................

.......................................................................

.......................................................................

.......................................................................

.......................................................................

.......................................................................

.......................................................................

# ONE DAY ONLY

Smudge this page with whatever
you are drinking right now.

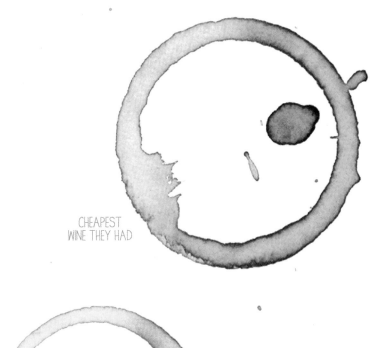

CHEAPEST
WINE THEY HAD

BEST COFFEE
I'VE EVER TASTED

Ask people you meet along your way to draw you a
map to a place they love in the neighborhood.

MAP:

NAME:

WHERE WE MET:

PLACE THEY LOVE:

MAP:

NAME: ........................................................................

WHERE WE MET: ........................................................................

PLACE THEY LOVE: ........................................................................

Try to find all of these colors over the course of your trip.
Record where you were when you found them and
what objects happened to be a perfect match.

| # | PLACE | DATE | OBJECT |
|---|-------|------|--------|
| | | | |
| | | | |
| | | | |
| | | | |
| | | | |
| | | | |
| | | | |
| | | | |
| | | | |
| | | | |
| | | | |
| | | | |
| | | | |
| | | | |
| | | | |
| | | | |
| | | | |
| | | | |
| | | | |
| | | | |
| | | | |
| | | | |
| | | | |
| | | | |
| | | | |

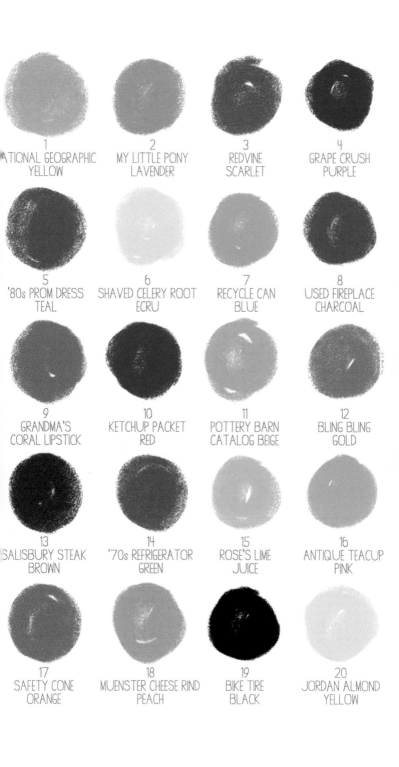

1
ATIONAL GEOGRAPHIC
YELLOW

2
MY LITTLE PONY
LAVENDER

3
REDVINE
SCARLET

4
GRAPE CRUSH
PURPLE

5
'80s PROM DRESS
TEAL

6
SHAVED CELERY ROOT
ECRU

7
RECYCLE CAN
BLUE

8
USED FIREPLACE
CHARCOAL

9
GRANDMA'S
CORAL LIPSTICK

10
KETCHUP PACKET
RED

11
POTTERY BARN
CATALOG BEIGE

12
BLING BLING
GOLD

13
SALISBURY STEAK
BROWN

14
'70s REFRIGERATOR
GREEN

15
ROSE'S LIME
JUICE

16
ANTIQUE TEACUP
PINK

17
SAFETY CONE
ORANGE

18
MUENSTER CHEESE RIND
PEACH

19
BIKE TIRE
BLACK

20
JORDAN ALMOND
YELLOW

Draw or list every item that is within your reach at this very moment. If objects are limited, expand to include interesting (or not-so-interesting) items within your line of sight.

MY SMALLEST-EVER
TRUSTY No. 2 PENCIL

✓ SMALLEST ITEM
✓ LARGEST ITEM
✓ MOST COLORFUL
✓ WEIRDEST SHAPE

Ask people you meet to share the recipe for an old-standby
meal that is cooked in their family often.

FROM THE KITCHEN OF:

WHAT'S COOKIN':

INGREDIENTS:

HOW TO MAKE:

FROM THE KITCHEN OF:

WHAT'S COOKIN':

INGREDIENTS:

HOW TO MAKE:

Keep your eyes peeled for textures that can
be collected and recorded as urban fossils.
Try taking rubbings of the following:

☐ city sewer grates
☐ the soles of shoes
☐ ornate building details
☐ local fauna
☐ bike tire tracks
☐ foreign currency
☐ subway tile

Storyboard interactions
you have with friends
or strangers.

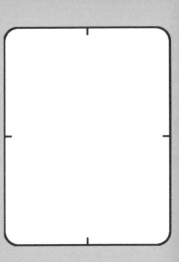

DATE: ...........................
SCENE: ...........................
.................................
.................................
.................................

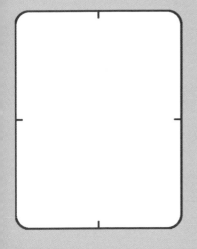

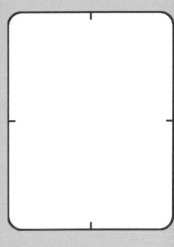

DATE: ...........................
SCENE: ...........................
...............................
...............................
...............................

DATE: ...........................
SCENE: ...........................
...............................
...............................
...............................

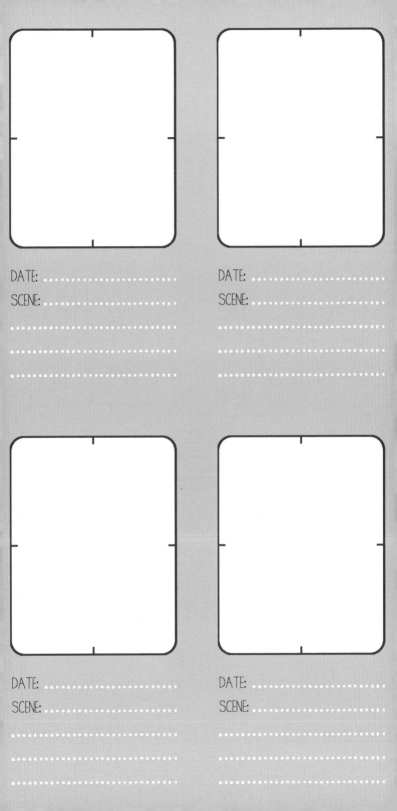

DATE: ........................

SCENE: ........................

........................

........................

........................

DATE: ........................

SCENE: ........................

........................

........................

........................

DATE: ........................

SCENE: ........................

........................

........................

........................

DATE: ........................

SCENE: ........................

........................

........................

........................

Take a Census. Record the answers to questions
you ask each stranger that you encounter along your way.

| QUESTION | PERSON #1 |
| --- | --- |
| WHAT DO YOU SPREAD ON TOAST? | |
| WHAT MAKES YOU HAPPY? | |
| WHAT TIME DO YOU WAKE UP? | |
| WHAT IS YOUR FAVORITE PLACE TO BE? | |
| WHAT IS YOUR FAVORITE TIME OF DAY? | |
| WHAT WAS YOUR FAVORITE AGE? | |
| HOW MANY JOBS HAVE YOU HAD? | |
| WHAT IS YOUR FAVORITE QUIET SPOT? | |
| WHERE DO YOU RENDEZVOUS WITH FRIENDS? | |
| HOW DO YOU GET AROUND TOWN? | |
| HOW MANY COUNTRIES HAVE YOU VISITED? | |
| HOW MANY... | |
| WHAT IS... | |
| | |
| | |
| | |
| | |
| | |
| | |
| | |

| ERSON #2 | PERSON #3 | PERSON #4 |
| --- | --- | --- |
| | | |
| | | |
| | | |
| | | |
| | | |
| | | |
| | | |
| | | |
| | | |
| | | |
| | | |
| | | |
| | | |
| | | |
| | | |
| | | |
| | | |
| | | |
| | | |
| | | |
| | | |

Look up.
What do you see from where you are sitting?

1.

2.

3.

4.

5.

6.

7.

8.

9.

10.

Record everyday objects
you come across that have
slightly different signage than
what you are familiar with.

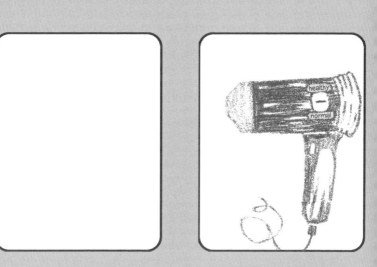

HEALTHY VS. NORMAL

SIEM REAP

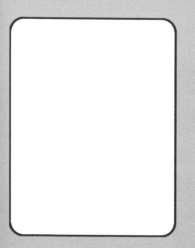

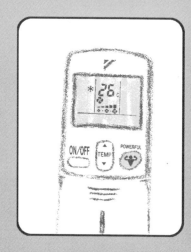

POWERFUL BUTTON

CHIANG MAI

KNOCK KNEED W.C.

HANOI

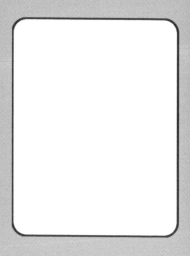

# IN THE FIELD

# & general city notes

3

$1

32955

6 7
5 6
4 5
3 4
2 3
1 2

96504

# FINDING YOUR BEARINGS

Airport: .......................................................

Airport Transport: .......................................................

Best Way To
Get Around This City: .......................................................

Train: .......................................................

Bus Line: .......................................................

Subway: .......................................................

Ferry: .......................................................

Taxi #: .......................................................

Home Base: .......................................................

Address: .......................................................

Phone #: .......................................................

Cross Streets: .......................................................

Subway/Bus Stop: .......................................................

Bike Rental: .......................................................

Scooter Rental: .......................................................

Car Share/Rental: .......................................................

Grocery Store: .......................................................

Nearest ATM: .......................................................

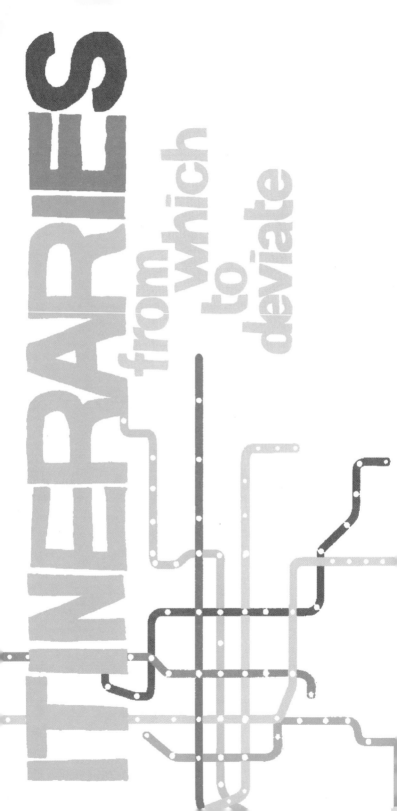

# ITINERARIES
## from which to deviate

Today's Weather: ☀ ⛅ ☁ 🌧

Date:

Place To Explore:

Things To See & Do:

- ☐
- ☐
- ☐
- ☐
- ☐
- ☐
- ☐
- ☐
- ☐
- ☐
- ☐
- ☐

Today's Weather: ☀ 🌤 ☁ 🌧

Date:

Place To Explore:

Things To See & Do:

- ☐ .............................................................
- ☐ .............................................................
- ☐ .............................................................
- ☐ .............................................................
- ☐ .............................................................
- ☐ .............................................................
- ☐ .............................................................
- ☐ .............................................................
- ☐ .............................................................
- ☐ .............................................................
- ☐ .............................................................
- ☐ .............................................................

Today's Weather:

Date:

Place To Explore:

Things To See & Do:

- [ ]
- [ ]
- [ ]
- [ ]
- [ ]
- [ ]
- [ ]
- [ ]
- [ ]
- [ ]
- [ ]
- [ ]

Today's Weather:

Date:

Place To Explore:

Things To See & Do:

- [ ] ....................................................
- [ ] ....................................................
- [ ] ....................................................
- [ ] ....................................................
- [ ] ....................................................
- [ ] ....................................................
- [ ] ....................................................
- [ ] ....................................................
- [ ] ....................................................
- [ ] ....................................................
- [ ] ....................................................
- [ ] ....................................................

........................................................
........................................................
........................................................
........................................................
........................................................
........................................................
........................................................
........................................................
........................................................

Today's Weather:

Date:

Place To Explore:

Things To See & Do:

☐ · · · · · · · · · · · · · · · · · · · · · · · · · · · · · · · · · · · · · · · · · · · · · · · · · · ·
☐ · · · · · · · · · · · · · · · · · · · · · · · · · · · · · · · · · · · · · · · · · · · · · · · · · · ·
☐ · · · · · · · · · · · · · · · · · · · · · · · · · · · · · · · · · · · · · · · · · · · · · · · · · · ·
☐ · · · · · · · · · · · · · · · · · · · · · · · · · · · · · · · · · · · · · · · · · · · · · · · · · · ·
☐ · · · · · · · · · · · · · · · · · · · · · · · · · · · · · · · · · · · · · · · · · · · · · · · · · · ·
☐ · · · · · · · · · · · · · · · · · · · · · · · · · · · · · · · · · · · · · · · · · · · · · · · · · · ·
☐ · · · · · · · · · · · · · · · · · · · · · · · · · · · · · · · · · · · · · · · · · · · · · · · · · · ·
☐ · · · · · · · · · · · · · · · · · · · · · · · · · · · · · · · · · · · · · · · · · · · · · · · · · · ·
☐ · · · · · · · · · · · · · · · · · · · · · · · · · · · · · · · · · · · · · · · · · · · · · · · · · · ·
☐ · · · · · · · · · · · · · · · · · · · · · · · · · · · · · · · · · · · · · · · · · · · · · · · · · · ·
☐ · · · · · · · · · · · · · · · · · · · · · · · · · · · · · · · · · · · · · · · · · · · · · · · · · · ·
☐ · · · · · · · · · · · · · · · · · · · · · · · · · · · · · · · · · · · · · · · · · · · · · · · · · · ·

Today's Weather: ☀ ⛅ ☁ 🌧

Date:

Place To Explore:

Things To See & Do:

- ☐ ......................................................
- ☐ ......................................................
- ☐ ......................................................
- ☐ ......................................................
- ☐ ......................................................
- ☐ ......................................................
- ☐ ......................................................
- ☐ ......................................................
- ☐ ......................................................
- ☐ ......................................................
- ☐ ......................................................
- ☐ ......................................................

......................................................
......................................................
......................................................
......................................................
......................................................
......................................................
......................................................
......................................................
......................................................

Today's Weather:

Date:

Place To Explore:

Things To See & Do:

- [ ] ....................................................
- [ ] ....................................................
- [ ] ....................................................
- [ ] ....................................................
- [ ] ....................................................
- [ ] ....................................................
- [ ] ....................................................
- [ ] ....................................................
- [ ] ....................................................
- [ ] ....................................................
- [ ] ....................................................
- [ ] ....................................................

....................................................
....................................................
....................................................
....................................................
....................................................
....................................................
....................................................
....................................................
....................................................
....................................................

# NEIGHBORHOODS

## to navigate & explore

## Neighborhood:

**Things To Observe:**

**Adventures To Have:**

**Places To Eat:**

**Places To Mingle:**

**Shops To Visit:**

**Streets To Check Out:**

**People To Talk To:**

## Neighborhood:

🔍 Things To Observe: ...........................................................
...........................................................................
...........................................................................

🧭 Adventures To Have: .........................................................
...........................................................................
...........................................................................

🍴 Places To Eat: ..............................................................
...........................................................................
...........................................................................

☕ Places To Mingle: ...........................................................
...........................................................................
...........................................................................

🏪 Shops To Visit: .............................................................
...........................................................................
...........................................................................

🪧 Streets To Check Out: .......................................................
...........................................................................
...........................................................................

💬 People To Talk To: ..........................................................
...........................................................................
...........................................................................

## Neighborhood:

**Things To Observe:**

**Adventures To Have:**

**Places To Eat:**

**Places To Mingle:**

OPEN **Shops To Visit:**

**Streets To Check Out:**

**People To Talk To:**

## Neighborhood:

🔍 **Things To Observe:**

🧭 **Adventures To Have:**

🍴 **Places To Eat:**

☕ **Places To Mingle:**

🪧 **Shops To Visit:**

🪧 **Streets To Check Out:**

💬 **People To Talk To:**

## Neighborhood:

🔍 Things To Observe:

🧭 Adventures To Have:

🍴 Places To Eat:

☕ Places To Mingle:

🏪 Shops To Visit:

🪧 Streets To Check Out:

💬 People To Talk To:

## Neighborhood:

Q Things To Observe: ................................................................

................................................................

................................................................

◎ Adventures To Have: ................................................................

................................................................

................................................................

🍴 Places To Eat: ................................................................

................................................................

................................................................

☕ Places To Mingle: ................................................................

................................................................

................................................................

🏷 Shops To Visit: ................................................................

................................................................

................................................................

🚏 Streets To Check Out: ................................................................

................................................................

................................................................

💬 People To Talk To: ................................................................

................................................................

................................................................

Things To Observe:

Adventures To Have:

Places To Eat:

Places To Mingle:

Shops To Visit:

Streets To Check Out:

People To Talk To:

RESTAURANTS
to enjoy
& review

323001

COFFEE    TEA    MILK

FOOD
BEVERAGE
SUB-TOTAL
TAX
TOTAL

Thank You!
Gracias!
Merci!
Danke!
有り難う

3230

## Place I Went:

☐ dive ☐ charming ☐ fancy pants

Tried The: .................................... ☐ yum ☐ yuck

.................................... ☐ yum ☐ yuck

.................................... ☐ yum ☐ yuck

The Secret
Ingredient Is: ....................................................

Don't Miss The: ....................................................

General
Thoughts: ....................................................

....................................................

....................................................

## Place I Went:

☐ dive ☐ charming ☐ fancy pants

Tried The: .................................... ☐ yum ☐ yuck

.................................... ☐ yum ☐ yuck

.................................... ☐ yum ☐ yuck

The Secret
Ingredient Is: ....................................................

Don't Miss The: ....................................................

General
Thoughts: ....................................................

....................................................

....................................................

## Place I Went:

☐ dive ☐ charming ☐ fancy pants

Tried The:
.......................................... ☐ yum ☐ yuck
.......................................... ☐ yum ☐ yuck
.......................................... ☐ yum ☐ yuck

The Secret
Ingredient Is:
..........................................

Don't Miss The:
..........................................

General
Thoughts:
..........................................
..........................................
..........................................

## Place I Went:

☐ dive ☐ charming ☐ fancy pants

Tried The:
.......................................... ☐ yum ☐ yuck
.......................................... ☐ yum ☐ yuck
.......................................... ☐ yum ☐ yuck

The Secret
Ingredient Is:
..........................................

Don't Miss The:
..........................................

General
Thoughts:
..........................................
..........................................
..........................................

## Place I Went:

☐ dive    ☐ charming    ☐ fancy pants

Tried The: ............................................    ☐ yum ☐ yuck
............................................    ☐ yum ☐ yuck
............................................    ☐ yum ☐ yuck

The Secret
Ingredient Is: ..................................................................

Don't Miss The: ..................................................................

General
Thoughts: ..................................................................
..................................................................
..................................................................


## Place I Went:

☐ dive    ☐ charming    ☐ fancy pants

Tried The: ............................................    ☐ yum ☐ yuck
............................................    ☐ yum ☐ yuck
............................................    ☐ yum ☐ yuck

The Secret
Ingredient Is: ..................................................................

Don't Miss The: ..................................................................

General
Thoughts: ..................................................................
..................................................................
..................................................................

## Place I Went:

☐ dive ☐ charming ☐ fancy pants

Tried The:
....................................... ☐ yum ☐ yuck
....................................... ☐ yum ☐ yuck
....................................... ☐ yum ☐ yuck

The Secret
Ingredient Is: .......................................

Don't Miss The: .......................................

General
Thoughts: .......................................
.......................................
.......................................

## Place I Went:

☐ dive ☐ charming ☐ fancy pants

Tried The:
....................................... ☐ yum ☐ yuck
....................................... ☐ yum ☐ yuck
....................................... ☐ yum ☐ yuck

The Secret
Ingredient Is: .......................................

Don't Miss The: .......................................

General
Thoughts: .......................................
.......................................
.......................................

Place I Went:

☐ dive      ☐ charming   ☐ fancy pants

Tried The: ........................................   ☐ yum ☐ yuck
........................................   ☐ yum ☐ yuck
........................................   ☐ yum ☐ yuck

The Secret
Ingredient Is: ........................................

Don't Miss The: ........................................

General
Thoughts: ........................................
........................................
........................................


Place I Went:

☐ dive      ☐ charming   ☐ fancy pants

Tried The: ........................................   ☐ yum ☐ yuck
........................................   ☐ yum ☐ yuck
........................................   ☐ yum ☐ yuck

The Secret
Ingredient Is: ........................................

Don't Miss The: ........................................

General
Thoughts: ........................................
........................................
........................................

ปลาร้า-ปลาช่อน

PICKLED
MUD FISH

SOY SAUCE   BALLPARK MUSTARD   KETCHUP   CURRY KETCHUP   HERB-Y OLIVE OIL   MALT VINEGAR

WASABI   CHILI OIL   MANGO PICKLE   MARMITE   SALSA

## Place I Went:

☐ dive        ☐ charming        ☐ fancy pants

Tried The: .................................................    ☐ yum  ☐ yuck
.................................................    ☐ yum  ☐ yuck
.................................................    ☐ yum  ☐ yuck

The Secret
Ingredient Is: .................................................

Don't Miss The: .................................................

General
Thoughts: .................................................

.................................................

.................................................

# REFER-ENCE
## & things that may come in handy

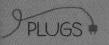 PLUGS

NORTH AMERICA, JAPAN,
TAIWAN & BRAZIL

EUROPE

DENMARK

ISRAEL

INDIA

FRANCE & BELGIUM

HONG KONG &
UNITED KINGDOM

AUSTRALIA
& CHINA

SWITZERLAND

ITALY

⚡ VOLTAGES ⚡

| | |
|---|---|
| Africa | 220–380 volts |
| Asia | 220 volts |
| Australia | 240 volts |
| Europe | 220 volts |
| India & Nepal | 220 volts |
| North America | 110 volts |
| South & Central America | 110–220 volts |
| Southeast Asia | 110–220 volts |
| United Kingdom | 240 volts |

# VARIOUS METRO SYMBOLS

 AMSTERDAM

 ATHENS

 ATLANTA

 BALTIMORE

 BANGKOK

 BOSTON

 BRASILIA

 BRUSSELS

 BUDAPEST

 BUENOS AIRES

 DUBLIN

 FORTALEZA

 GLASGOW

 GUADALAJARA

 HAIFA

 ISTANBUL

 LISBON

 LIVERPOOL

 LONDON

 LOS ANGELES

 MEXICO CITY

 MIAMI

 MONTREAL

 MOSCOW

 NEW JERSEY

 PORTLAND

 PRAGUE

 RIO DE JANEIRO

 ROME

 SAN FRANCISCO

 ST. LOUIS

 STOCKHOLM

 ST. PETERSBURG

 SYDNEY

TAIPEI

marta
BTS
Subte
DART
UNDERGROUND
CityRail

92

 BARCELONA

 BEIJING

 BERLIN

 BILBAO

 CAIRO

 CARACAS

 CHICAGO

 COPENHAGEN

DELHI

 HELSINKI

 HIROSHIMA

 HONG KONG

 ICHEON

 MADRID

 MANILA

 MARACAIBO

 MEDELLIN

 MELBOURNE

 NEW YORK

 OSAKA

 OSLO

 PARIS

 PHILADELPHIA

 SÃO PAULO

 SEOUL

 SF BAY AREA

 SHANGHAI

 SINGAPORE

 TEHRAN

 TOKYO

 WARSAW

 WASHINGTON

# RULERS & CONVERSIONS

## LENGTH
1 inch = 25.4 millimeters
1 inch = 2.54 centimeters
1 inch = 0.025 meters
1 foot = 12 inches
1 foot = 0.3 meters
1 yard = 3 feet
1 yard = 0.91 meters
1 mile = 1.61 kilometers

## AREA
1 sq. foot = 144 sq. inches
1 sq. foot = 0.09 sq. meters
1 sq. yard = 9 sq. feet
1 acre = 4840 sq. yards
1 sq. mile = 640 acres

## CAPACITY
1 ounce = 29.57 milliliters
1 cup = 236.59 milliliters
1 pint = 16 ounces
1 pint = 2 cups
1 quart = 2 pints
1 gallon = 4 quarts

## WEIGHT
1 pound = 16 ounces
1 pound = 453.6 grams
1 ounce = 28.35 grams
1 short ton = 2,000 pounds
1 short ton = 0.91 metric tons

# MEN'S
## SHIRT COLLAR

| | | | | | | |
|---|---|---|---|---|---|---|
| U.S.A. | 15 | 15.5 | 16 | 16.5 | 17 | 17.5 |
| U.K. | 15 | 15.5 | 16 | 16.5 | 17 | 17.5 |
| Europe | 38 | 39 | 40 | 41 | 42 | 43 |
| Australia | 38 | 39 | 40 | 41 | 42 | 43 |
| Japan | 38 | 39 | 40 | 41 | 42 | 43 |

## JACKETS

| | | | | | | |
|---|---|---|---|---|---|---|
| U.S.A. | 35 | 36 | 37 | 38 | 39 | 40 |
| U.K. | 35 | 36 | 37 | 38 | 39 | 40 |
| Europe | 46 | 48 | 50 | 52 | 54 | 56 |
| Australia | 92 | 96 | 100 | 104 | 108 | 112 |
| Japan | S | | M | | L | |

## SHOES

| | | | | | | |
|---|---|---|---|---|---|---|
| U.S.A. | 6.5 | 7.5 | 8.5 | 9.5 | 10.5 | 11.5 |
| U.K. | 6 | 7 | 8 | 9 | 10 | 11 |
| Europe | 40 | 41 | 42 | 43 | 44.5 | 46 |
| Australia | 6 | 7 | 8 | 9 | 10 | 11 |
| Japan | 25 | 26 | 27.5 | 28 | 29 | 30 |

# WOMEN'S
## SHIRTS

| | | | | | | |
|---|---|---|---|---|---|---|
| U.S.A. | 6 | 8 | 10 | 12 | 14 | 16 |
| U.K. | 32 | 34 | 36 | 38 | 40 | 42 |
| Japan | S | | M | | L | |

## DRESSES

| | | | | | | |
|---|---|---|---|---|---|---|
| U.S.A. | 6 | 8 | 10 | 12 | 14 | 16 |
| U.K. | 8 | 10 | 12 | 14 | 16 | 18 |
| Europe | 36 | 38 | 40 | 42 | 44 | 46 |
| Australia | 8 | 10 | 12 | 14 | 16 | 18 |
| Japan | 5 | 7 | 9 | 11 | 13 | 15 |

## SHOES

| | | | | | | |
|---|---|---|---|---|---|---|
| U.S.A. | 6.5 | 7 | 7.5 | 8 | 8.5 | 9 |
| U.K. | 5 | 5.5 | 6 | 6.5 | 7 | 7.5 |
| Europe | 37 | 37 | 38 | 38 | 39 | 39 |
| France only | 37 | 38 | 38 | 39 | 39 | 40 |
| Australia | 6.5 | 7 | 7.5 | 8 | 8.5 | 9 |
| Japan | 23.5 | 24 | 24.5 | 25 | 25.5 | 26 |

# A BIT OF TRANSLATION

| ENGLISH | FRENCH | SPANISH | GERMAN |
|---------|--------|---------|--------|
| Hello | Bonjour | Hola | Hallo |
| Goodbye | Au revoir | Adios | Auf wiedersehen |
| Yes | Oui | Sí | Ja |
| No | Non | No | Nein |
| Please | S'il vous plaît | Por favor | Bitte |
| Thank you | Merci | Gracias | Danke |
| You're welcome | De rien | De nada | Bitte |
| Excuse me | Excusez-moi | Perdón | Entschuldigung |
| My name is | Je m'appelle | Me llamo | Mein name ist |
| How much? | Combien? | ¿Cuánto? | Wie viel? |
| Where is | Où est | Dónde está | Wo ist |
| The toilet | La toilette | El baño | Die toilette |
| A room | Une chambre | Un cuarto | Ein zimmer |

# SOME PICTORIAL SIGN LANGUAGE

## ESSENTIALS

## TRANSPORT

| JAPANESE | MANDARIN | ITALIAN | HINDI |
|---|---|---|---|
| Konnichiwa | Ni hao | Buon giorno | Namaste |
| Sayonara | Zaijian | Arrivederci | Alvida |
| Hai | Dui | Sì | Haa |
| Iie | Bu | No | Nahee |
| Dozo | Qing | Per piacere | Kripaya |
| Domo arigato | Xie xie | Grazie | Dhanyavaad |
| Do itashimashite | Bu ke qi | Prego | Apaka svagata hai |
| Sumimasen | Duibuqi | Scusi | Maaf keejie |
| Watashi wa | Wo shi | Mi chiamo | Mera naam |
| Ikura? | Duo shao? | Quanto? | Kitana? |
| Doko desu ka | Zai nali | Dove é | Kaham hai |
| Toire | Cesuo | Il gabinetto | Saucalaya |
| Heya | Yi shi | Una camera | Eka kamara |

# CLOUD IDENTIFICATION

CIRROCUMULUS

CIRRUS

— 20,000 FEET

ALTOCUMULUS

— 6,500 FEET

ALTOSTRATUS

STRATOCUMULUS

## TEMPERATURE

| F | 32 | 41 | 50 | 59 | 68 | 86 | 100 |
|---|----|----|----|----|----|----|-----|
| C | 0 | 5 | 10 | 15 | 20 | 30 | 38 |

COLD FRONT

WARM FRONT

STATIONARY

OCCLUDED

CUMULONIMBUS

CUMULUS

STRATUS

NIMBOSTRATUS

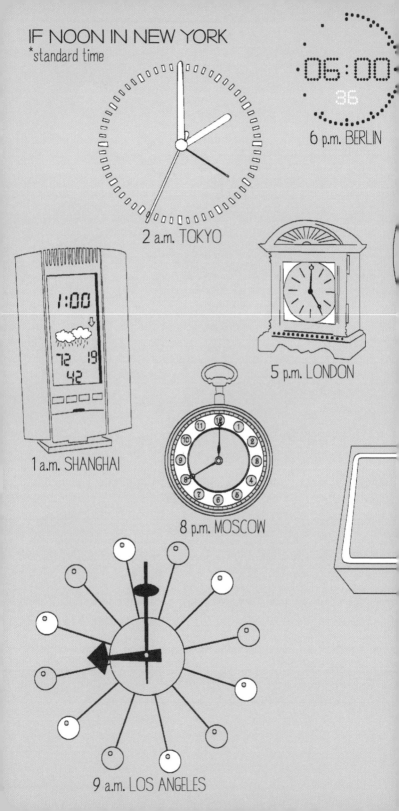

IF NOON IN NEW YORK
*standard time

6 p.m. BERLIN

2 a.m. TOKYO

5 p.m. LONDON

1 a.m. SHANGHAI

8 p.m. MOSCOW

9 a.m. LOS ANGELES

12 a.m. HANOI

10:30 p.m. NEW DEHLI

2 p.m. BUENOS AIRES

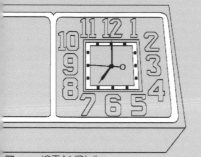
7 p.m. ISTANBUL

3 a.m. SYDNEY

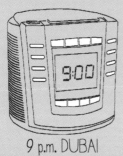
9 p.m. DUBAI

# INTERNATIONAL DUMPLING TYPES

| | |
|---|---|
| Africa | fufu |
| Armenia | manti (with sour cream) |
| Austria | napkin dumpling |
| Bahamas | guava duff |
| China | jiaozi, wonton & a million other varieties |
| China-Shanghai | xiaolongbao (there's soup inside) |
| Czech Republic | pirohy |
| Dominican Republic | domplin |
| Eastern Europe | kreplach |
| England-Dorset | doughboy |
| Georgia | khinkali |
| Germany | klopse |
| Hungary | cabbage dumpling |
| India | samosa |
| Italy | ravioli & tortellini |
| Japan | gyoza & takoyaki (octopus dumpling) |
| Korea | mandu |
| Latin America | tamale (in corn husk or plantain leaf) |
| Lithuania | cepelinai |
| Mongolia | buuz |
| Nepal | momo |
| Norway | poteball, klubb, raspeball, komperdose, ruta |
| Peru | papas rellenas (with onion/lime sauce) |
| Philippines | siomai |
| Poland | pierogi |
| Russia | pelmeni |
| Scotland | clootie dumpling |
| Siberia | pozi |
| Sweden-Northern | pitepalt (with lingonberry jam) |
| Sweden-Southern | kroppkaka (with cream or lingonberry jam) |
| Thailand | sticky rice dumpling (in banana leaf) |
| Turkey | manti (with yogurt & red pepper powder) |
| Ukraine | vareniki |
| United States | chicken & dumplin' |

CLOOTIE DUMPLING
(Scotland)

STICKY RICE DUMPLING
(Thailand)

SIOMAI
(Philippines)

XIAOLONGBAO
(Shanghai)

RAVIOLI
(Italy)

TAMALE
(Latin America)

TAKOYAKI
(Japan)

KREPLACH
(Eastern Europe)

MANDU
(Korea)

PITEPALT
(Northern Sweden)

# VARIOUS INTERNATIONAL COFFEE & TEA TRADITIONS

VIETNAMESE
COFFEE
(with condensed milk)

MAYAN COFFEE
(cinnamon, cayenne
cocoa & cream)

ARABIC
COFFEE
(with cardamom)

ITALIAN
ESPRESSO
(drink quickly)

NEW YORK
ICED COFFEE
(giant sized in the
summer time)

NEW ORLEANS
COFFEE
(chicory)

CHILEAN HELADO
(Chantilly cream,
dulce de leche &
ground almonds)

PORTLAND
CAPPUCCINO
(fancy pants
artisanal)

INDONESIAN COFFEE
(with soda &
sweetened
condensed milk)

YEMENESE COFFEE
(with ginger)

CANADIAN COFFEE
(always fresh)

AUSTRALIAN
SWEET MILK COFFEE
(milk only, no water)

**THAI ICED TEA**
(with tamarind &
condensed milk,
served in a
plastic bag)

**TURKISH CAY**
(drink with a sugar
cube behind your teeth)

**INDIAN MASALA CHAI**
(spiced milky tea)

**TIBETAN PO CHA**
(smokey black tea,
salt, yak butter & milk)

**JAPANESE
MATCHA**
(powdered
green tea)

**TAIWANESE BOBA**
(flavored milk tea
with tapioca &
a huge, fat straw)

**BRITISH TEA**
(black tea with
cream & sugar)

**RUSSIAN TEA**
(served in a
podstakannik)

**ARGENTINIAN
YERBA MATTE**
(will keep you up)

**EGYPTIAN KOSHARY**
(black tea with cane
sugar & mint)

**CHINESE OOLONG**
(partially oxidized)

**KENTUCKY
SWEET TEA**
(with a lot of ice)

**AFRICAN ROOIBOS**
(naturally sweet
red tea)

**MOROCCAN TEA**
(green tea with mint)

**HONG KONG
LEMON TEA**
(muddle the lemon)

**KOREAN ROASTED
BARLEY TEA**
(hot or iced)

# NOTES

## observations, stories, & encounters & collected miscellany

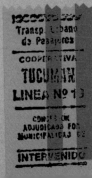

N. 1 ADULT

EUR ✗✗✗✗ 4.36

P.IVA 403151003

DOWNTOWN
◄ OUTBOUND ►

## PROHIBITED OUTFITS

"TAXI!"

BUSY

OFF DUTY

From _____

To _____

ARRIVED

Date    Train    Time

DELIVERED

Date    Time

H 64589